# Reduce, Reuse, Recycle

# Glass

Alexandra Fix

Heinemann Library
Chicago, Illinois

Customer Service  888-454-2279
Visit our website at www.heinemannraintree.com

Designed by Steven Mead and Debbie Oatley
Illustration by Jeff Edwards
Printed in China by South China Printing Company Limited

12 11 10 09 08
10 9 8 7 6 5 4 3 2

10-digit ISBNs: 1-4034-9718-4 (hc)  1-4034-9726-5 (pb)

**Library of Congress Cataloging-in-Publication Data**
Fix, Alexandra, 1950-
  Glass / Alexandra Fix.
    p. cm. -- (Reduce, reuse, recycle)
  Includes bibliographical references and index.
  ISBN 978-1-4034-9718-5 (hc) -- ISBN 978-1-4034-9726-0 (pb)
  1.  Glass waste--Recycling--Juvenile literature. I. Title.
  TD799.F59 2007
  666'.14--dc22
                          2007002791

**Acknowledgments**
The author and publisher are grateful to the following for permission to reproduce copyright material: Alamy pp. **4** (Gastrofotos), **5** (Ace Stock Limited), **6** (Foodfolio), **7** (Fstop2/Keith Pritchard), **10** (David Hoffman Photo Library), **11** (Robert Brook), **12** (Mark Boulton), **13** (Eddie Gerald), **16** (Matt Cardy), **17** (Tetra Images), **18** (Bob Purdue), **19** (Craig Holmes), **20** (Kim Karpeles), **23** (ImageState/Pictor International), **25** (Image100), **27** (Colin Hugill); Corbis pp. **8** (Kazuyoshi Nomachi), **9** (Sandro Vannini), **21** (Philip James Corwin), **24** (Erika Koch/Zefa); Harcourt Education Ltd. pp. **15** (Ginny Stroud-Lewis), **26** (Ginny Stroud-Lewis); Science Photo Library pp. **14** (Martin Bond), **22** (Hank Morgan).

Cover photograph reproduced with permission of Corbis/Franc Enskat/zefa.

# Contents

Some words are shown in bold, **like this**. You can find out what they mean by looking in the glossary.

# What Is Glass Waste?

Glass is a strong, clear material that is used to make items such as windows, bottles, and containers. Glass is a useful material, but sometimes it is wasted.

Food items are often stored in glass jars.

Glass waste ends up at **landfills** with other materials.

Glass waste is glass that is thrown away. If glass is reused or **recycled**, it can be used over and over again.

# What Is Made of Glass?

Many foods and drinks are stored in glass bottles. Plates, cups, drinking glasses, and cookware are often made of glass. Pottery is sometimes **glazed** with a thin layer of glass.

↑ Food items such as vinegar are kept in glass bottles.

Some boats are made of fiberglass.
Fiberglass is a mixture of glass and plastic.

Small items such as lightbulbs are made of glass. Large items such as windows, mirrors, and some doors are also made of glass.

# Where Does Glass Come From?

Glass is made from sand, soda ash, and lime. Sand comes from **dunes**, beaches, and the ocean floor. Lime is removed from limestone rock. Soda ash comes from a mineral rock called trona.

Sand is rock that has broken into tiny pieces over time.

Melted glass can be formed into many shapes while it is hot.

Glass is made in **factories**. The sand, soda ash, and lime are melted and made into glass. **Fuels** such as coal, oil, or natural gas are used to heat the mixture.

# Will We Always Have Glass?

↑ Sand is an important ingredient in glass.

Sand, lime, and soda ash are **nonrenewable resources**. Once these materials are used up, they will be gone forever.

We use other nonrenewable resources as **fuel** to make glass. These include oil, coal, and natural gas. Every time we make new glass, we use up some of these fuels.

Glass **factories** can cause harmful air **pollution**.

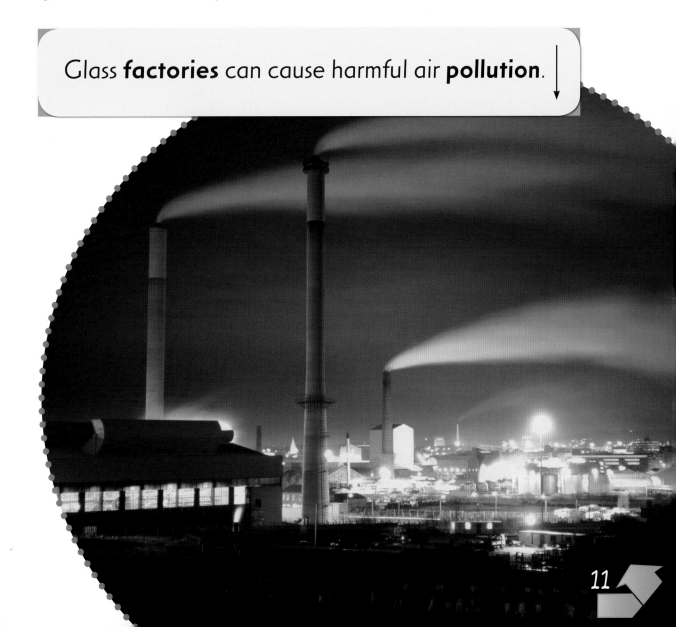

# What Happens When We Waste Glass?

When glass is thrown away, it is brought to a **landfill**. Tons of glass are buried in landfills. Glass bottles in a landfill could take up to a million years to rot away.

People throw away many tons of glass every year.
→

Bright sun shining through glass litter can start grass fires.

Glass **litter** is dangerous. People and animals can get cut by broken glass pieces. Mosquitoes can lay their eggs in glass bottles and spread diseases.

# How Can We Reduce Glass Waste?

The best way to reduce glass waste is to use less glass. Try not to buy glass items that you do not need. Ask your family to buy glass items that last a long time, such as energy-saving lightbulbs.

Energy-saving lightbulbs have to be replaced less often than regular lightbulbs.

Many household glass bottles can be **recycled**.

Try not to buy drinks that come in glass bottles. Instead, reuse a drink container from home. You can fill it with water or juice from home or refill your drink at a water fountain.

# How Can We Reuse Glass?

There are many ways to reuse glass. You can give unwanted glass items to stores that sell used things. Other people might have a good use for your old mirrors, dishes, or drinking glasses.

Some companies mix used glass into concrete blocks.

A glass jar is handy for storing paintbrushes.

Think of new ways to reuse glass jars.
One could hold a shell collection.
Another could hold homemade cookies.
Decorate a skinny jar to use as a vase.

# How Can We Recycle Glass?

When glass is **recycled**, it is melted down and used again to make a new item. Most **communities** have a recycling program for glass, paper, plastic, and metal.

Many cities and towns have recycling bins in public places.

The only glass items that can be recycled from home are glass bottles and jars. After you have saved these items, rinse them out and remove any caps.

Only clear, brown, or green glass can be recycled.

——→

# Where Can We Bring Glass for Recycling?

Some cities and towns have **recycling** programs. People can leave recycling bins outside their homes. A truck picks up the items and brings them to a recycling center.

Glass, metal, and plastic items must be separated from paper.

Some **communities** use fun ways to remind us to recycle.

You can also bring used glass to a recycling center or grocery store. From there, it is taken to a **factory**. Then it is made into recycled glass.

# How Is Glass Recycled?

After glass is brought to a **recycling** center, it is sorted by color. Then it is sent to a glass **factory**. There it is crushed into tiny pieces, called cullet.

Crushed glass (cullet) is washed to remove glue and food particles.

Glass can be recycled over and over again.

Cullet is added to liquid glass in a **furnace**. The mixture is made into new glass objects.

# How Do We Use Recycled Glass?

**Recycled** glass is safe to use for making new food and drink containers. Tiny glass pieces are used on sandpaper and for **sandblasting**.

Old glass bottles can be recycled to make new glass bottles.

At night, glass pieces in the paint make the lines look brighter. ↑

Finely crushed glass can go into **asphalt** for playgrounds and roads. It is also added to the paint used to draw the yellow lines on roads.

# How Can You Take Action?

You can help reduce glass waste. Ask friends and family to start **recycling** glass. You can help by washing out bottles and removing the caps.

Use leftover dishwater to rinse bottles for recycling.

# Reduce

# Reuse

# Recycle

Your design here

LUCKY WINNERS
EACH WILL
WIN A
WASTE AWARE
ABERDEENSHIRE
GOODIE BAG

It takes less energy to reuse or recycle glass than it does to make new glass.

Ask an adult to help you find your local recycling center. Make a recycling poster to hang at school. By reducing glass waste, we can help keep our planet clean.

# Make a Bug Jar

**Ask an adult to help you with this project.**

You can create your own bug jar by using an old glass container. Follow the steps below.

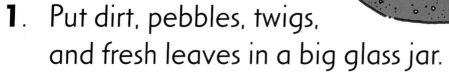

1. Put dirt, pebbles, twigs, and fresh leaves in a big glass jar.
2. Add a little moss or crumpled tissue paper to make a bug hiding space.
3. Put water in a small lid and set it in the jar.
4. Punch holes in the jar lid for air.

5. Catch or buy two crickets.
6. Feed the crickets bits of fruit, vegetables, green leaves, tropical fish flakes, or dry cat food.

You now have a bug jar! Check on your bug everyday and write down what you see.

# Fast Facts

Most glass bottles and jars are made of some **recycled** glass.

The windows in cars are made of layers of glass and plastic. They will not break into sharp pieces.

Glass never wears out. It can be recycled over and over again.

# Glossary

| | |
|---|---|
| **asphalt** | mixture of sand, gravel, and tar used to make roads, parking lots, and other hard surfaces |
| **community** | group of people who live in one area |
| **dune** | hill of sand found on coasts and in deserts |
| **factory** | building or buildings where something is made |
| **fuel** | material that is burned to create power or heat |
| **furnace** | closed-off space that is heated at high temperatures to warm a building or to melt solid materials |
| **glaze** | cover with a thin layer of glass |
| **landfill** | large area where trash is dumped, crushed, and covered with soil |
| **litter** | trash |
| **nonrenewable resource** | material of the earth that cannot be replaced by nature |
| **pollution** | wastes and poisons in the air, water, or soil |
| **recycle** | break down a material and use it again to make a new product. Recycling is the act of breaking down a material and using it again. |
| **sandblasting** | cleaning a surface with sand and tiny pieces of glass that are pushed by a strong blast of air |

# Find Out More

## Books to Read

Firestone, Mary. *Glass*. Mankato, MN: Capstone Press, 2005.

Galko, Francine. *Earth Friends at Home*. Chicago: Heinemann Library, 2004.

Oxlade, Chris. *How We Use Glass*. Chicago: Raintree, 2004.

## Web Sites

The Environmental Protection Agency works to protect the air, water, and land. The organization has a special Web site for students at www.epa.gov/kids.

Earth911 is an organization that gives information about where you can recycle in your community. Their Web site for students is http://www.earth911.org/master.asp?s=kids&a=kids/kids.asp.

# Index